KRISTINA CLEMENS

THE CHIC GIRL'S GUIDE

TO A ONE-OF-A-KIND WARDROBE

ALTERING AND EMBELLISHING HEMLINES, SLEEVES, AND MORE

PLAIN SIGHT PUBLISHING
AN IMPRINT OF CEDAR FORT, INC.
SPRINGVILLE, UTAH

ISBN 13: 978-1-4621-1246-3

Published by Plain Sight Publishing, an imprint of Cedar Fort, Inc.
2373 W. 700 S., Springville, UT 84663
Distributed by Cedar Fort, Inc., www.cedarfort.com

LIBRARY OF CONGRESS CATALOGING-IN-PUBLICATION DATA

Clemens, Kristina, author.
  The chic girl's guide to a one-of-a-kind wardrobe : altering and embellishing hemlines, sleeves, and more / Kristina Clemens.
    pages cm
  Includes bibliographical references and index.
  1. Clothing and dress--Alteration. I. Title.

  TT550.C54 2013
  646'.3--dc23
                              2013017091

Cover and page design by Angela D. Olsen
Cover design © 2013 by Lyle Mortimer
Edited by Whitney A. Lindsley

Printed in the United States of America

10 9 8 7 6 5 4 3 2 1

To my mom—

whose vibrant creativity inspires me every time
I approach my sewing machine

Contents

Foreword

In 2007 I started posting daily outfits on my blog *Clothed Much*. It began as an online outfit diary to help me be creative with what I already had and evolved into a modest fashion blog after I realized how little modesty and fashion were linked and discussed. A common misconception seems to exist that you can't be modest *and* stylish, as if you only had the choice to be one and not the other. *Clothed Much* is my attempt to counter this generalization with outfits, styling tips, tutorials, and guest bloggers discussing their personal views.

As a woman, I understand how frustrating it is to shop for clothing that fits properly and covers you comfortably. That's where refashioning and DIY style comes in. I'll admit I'm not the best when it comes to refashioning. If you give me a tutorial, of course I'll do my best to follow it, but it'll definitely look like a kindergarten project. I'll even hang it up on my fridge to showcase my beautiful work!

Kristina, on the other hand, has a knack for taking something dull and turning it into something *fabulous*. This is what attracted me to her and convinced me that I absolutely needed her perspective on *Clothed Much*. Her tutorials and DIY projects are much loved because they're easy and on-trend!

Even if you're not a self-proclaimed modest fashionista, I'm sure you've seen tops or dresses on which the neckline was too low for your taste or perhaps not as work-appropriate as you need, or maybe you bought a skirt on a whim that was shorter than you were used to wearing. This book can help with all of that (and more). Next time you're hesitant to buy those great pieces because you're afraid you can't make them work for your body and lifestyle, you'll have these techniques to guide you in turning them into more wearable garments.

Elaine Hearn
fashion blogger

Acknowledgments

Thank you, God, for keeping your promises.

Scott, problem solver, best friend, tireless supporter, and most importantly . . . Studhubs—you help me embrace the adventure of each new day.

My enthusiastic blog readers—for challenging me to keep posting DIY projects by returning again and again. You are the humbling ground, my friends.

Haley Miller – for discovering my tutorials online and seeing the potential for a book. One word: Thanks

Thanks to Elaine Hearn, who opened clothedmuch.com to contributors and generated more publicity for my sewing projects than I ever could on my own.

Thanks also to my beautiful models—Katelyn Sproles, Kayla Graf, and Sarah Wells— for their willingness and general loveliness. You make my book purdy!

And finally, thanks to the individuals whose passion for DIY makes books like this worthwhile.

I salute you. Rock on.

Introduction

Why write a book of sewing projects?

I've pondered this. It's not that I don't enjoy sewing and design. I tweet about it. I write a blog about it. I *love* it. But honestly, what sort of technique could I possibly demonstrate that hasn't already been addressed by every craft blogger, seamstress, and DIY style maven out there?

I go back to that bright, spring day as a fourteen-year-old when that longing bloomed—back to the moment when I realized I desperately wanted to be able to create a version of the fantastic garments seen in stores that actually fit my body and lifestyle. It was agony to gaze into a store window at the gauzy, chiffon dress of my dreams that was, hello—about six inches too short. I was plagued by visions of glamorous pieces with unattainable price points and even more disappointed by the offerings available at Goodwill in every size but my own. Visions of dresses with ruffles and girly details danced in my head and the desire to create beautiful, wearable garments was indescribable. It wasn't something I wanted to do; it was something I needed to do.

I was blessed to be raised by parents who encouraged the creativity inside me to be developed, with a mom who could sew anything and a dad who could build everything. "I can fix that" was the slogan of my family, so it never occurred to me to be intimidated by short hemlines or sleeveless dresses. My first foray into sewing had been a perfectly horrid drawstring skirt constructed from the stiffest fabric ever woven, which I entered into a 4-H competition when I was ten. The skirt suffered some unremembered fate, but that experience sparked a compulsive desire inside me to nip, tuck, and reconstruct anything I could get my hands on. I distinctly remember the trips to the fabric store, where my mother taught me the basics of good design—matching the colors, choosing the silhouettes, and balancing the proportions. For me, a deliciously fantastic dress was always as close as the nearest fabric store and my mother's sewing machine.

Unfortunately, refashioning and upcycling was decidedly unchic back then. There was no Etsy. No Project Runway. No DIY section in the magazines. A how-to guide of innovative tips for the modern stitcher had yet to be written, so armed with only inner creativity and my mom's sewing know-how, I set out to create. As a budding seamstress, I found the best inspiration for DIY style projects could be found from what was missing in store-bought clothes. Short skirts and plunging necklines induced a frenetic parade of ideas in my mind, and I spent hours dreaming up ideas on how to fill the empty space. After years of experimental projects (think the good, the bad, and the ugly), I ironed out the kinks and put together a group of techniques to help you blend the whimsical with the wearable.

In *The Chic Girl's Guide* (that's *chic*, like the Arabian *sheikh*—not the Chiclet variety), you'll find creative techniques designed to inspire you to adjust your hemlines, play with sleeve additions, and add height to necklines in novel ways; and any of these projects can be customized to fit your signature style. This book is designed to become the tool you need to create garments that have a flattering fit, feminine detailing, and are utterly unique—designer duds at Target prices, as I like to say. *The Chic Girl's Guide* is like a free fall into a universe where your creativity can flourish and materialize with the application of stylish solutions to create a one-of-a-kind wardrobe.

I am writing this book for me, for the younger version of myself, and for you . . . sharing the ideas I wish someone had shared with me, revealing the techniques that could have saved me hours of tears and frustration while trying to refashion garments that proved you could, you know . . . beautify without looking gimmicky. This is workbook of tutorials, tips, and guidelines on how to customize and embellish, but at its core, this is a book of ideas meant to inspire young and old alike—to shine a light on the possibilities of revamping store-bought clothes into garments that can be as quirky and classy and girly as you want them to be.

And that, my dears, is why I've written a book of sewing projects.

The Chic Girl's List of Supplies

Thousands of trendy and amazing supplies are available to the refashionista, but since this isn't *The Chic Girl's Guide to Stand out Sewing Tools*, I've listed only the materials you'll need for the projects demonstrated in this book. (You're welcome.)

Elastic—for nipping in those baggy bits. I used ½-inch to 2-inch widths.

Fabric—not optional, sorry . . . though you're welcome to try. That would be very "The Emperor's New Clothes" of you.

Fabric Cutting Machine—This one's optional, but it could be argued that the time and energy it saves could have the same health benefits as eating a small apple a day. My favorite choice is the Sizzix Big Shot, which costs a lot less than other fabric cutters. Note: Only the Originals BIGZ dies will work on fabric.

Fadeaway marker pens—convenient for marking seam placement or flowers. The ink fades in 48 hours, but test on a scrap of your fabric first.

Glue gun—because thread won't hold everything in place.

Iron and ironing board—essential if you want your finished product to look professional. Many a good project has been sidelined by lack of a good ironing.

Measurements—Take a few measurements: waist, torso length, and skirt length. To get an accurate waist measurement, measure around the waist an inch or so above your belly button.

For torso length, have a family member or friend measure from the base of the back of your neck down to the where you want the hem of your clothes to fall.

Take another measurement from your belly button to the same point on your legs to determine skirt length.

My minimum dress measurement is 40 inches.

My minimum skirt measurement for a skirt that sits at the natural waist is 25 inches.

These two measurements are what I call the comfort zone. It's the approximate finished length I'm comfortable with wearing and the number I use when calculating for DIY projects.

40 in. 25 in

DRESS LENGTH SKIRT LENGTH

The Comfort Zone

Knowing your personal measurements will make it easier to analyze the possibilities of any given item of clothing. It's also helpful to know the most common measurement for a store-bought dress these days is 35 to 38 inches. A skirt from my favorite online store with a finished measurement of 21 inches gives me four inches of empty space to embellish. If a dress is only 30 inches long, I know I'm looking at the possibility of major dress surgery. Having this knowledge makes it easy when shopping in stores or online to evaluate how much empty space I have to play with when applying modifications.

Needle and thread—Gotta have 'em. A small fine-point needle will serve you well for the projects in this book. You will also need a spool of clear thread.

Pincushion—Nifty for keeping all your pins in the same place and the sharp edges away from your crafty little fingers.

Safety pins—You'll need the extra-large size to pull elastic through a garment facing.

Scissors—unless you have a talent for rending things with your teeth, invest in a good pair of fabric scissors.

Seam ripper—it's your new best friend. A nifty little tool to help you rip out mistakes (which you'll never need to use because you're awesome like that).

Sewing machine—unless you're seriously into hand stitching .

Sewing machine needles—the most-overlooked tool by novice sewers. Having the suitable machine needle for the type of fabric you're using will eliminate tons . . . no, *TONS* of frustration. For starters, universal or ballpoint needles will work well for most fabrics.

Straight pins—If you pin before sewing, you're projects will just look better. I promise.

Snaps and Snap Kit—Buy the corresponding kit that goes with the size snap you choose

Tape measure—Use it, use it, use it! (Note: Use it.)

Thimble (*or as my daughter would say: "Look, Mom . . . a tiny trash can!"*)—Again, optional. But a thimble can be mighty handy when pushing a needle through several layers of fabric and it's always nice *not* to puncture your thumb with a needle. Just sayin'.

Various rhinestones, paillettes, sequins, and buttons—Garments just look prettier with them.

Yardstick—A handy tool to help keep a straight line when cutting long sections of fabric.

Chic Girl's Tip

Use ballpoint needles when sewing on stretchy knit fabrics to avoid seams that look like a stretched-out mess.

From Inspiration to Execution

Getting the most from this book

Start with the pictures. Within this book, there's a wide range of fashion projects for girls who love time-intensive labors of love as well as those who prefer a craft on the go. Rustle through the pages until a picture catches your eye. Pause and consider what it is that sparks your imagination, then formulate an idea of how you want a particular garment to look and the role you want it to play in your wardrobe. Think it through: these are the choices I've been given and here's what I could do with it. Your ability to analyze a garment objectively gets easier with practice.

Chic Girl's Tip

Envision the possibilities. Whether it's sweetly loopy, super smart, or vintage inspired, the hallmark of a great refashion is that first, you can't look away from the awesomeness, and second, you keep wondering "Did she do that herself or did it come like that"?

The tone of the finished product is only limited by your imagination, and whether you wear it confidently is limited only by your own insecurities. I've met girls who re-fashion clothes in the most amazing ways, then never wear them—like, never ever—because they're afraid someone will ask if they altered it. Let's face it. If you boldly take a garment from yawn-fest to swoon-worthy, it *will* incite a certain amount of curiosity. Should the people you meet have an eye for detail and appreciate the designer flare you've put into your clothes, *bonus*.

One last thing.

Don't worry about messing up. Failure to realize your original idea can take a project to unexpected places and open your mind to new possibilities. Every flaw is a lesson learned, every mistake—innovation in disguise. Look for the *Chic Girl's Tips*, where you'll get an inside look into my creative process, personal cheats, and extra tidbits to take your projects beyond the common pitfalls of DIY style. Evaluate color, shape, and fabric; then embrace the task at hand. Approach each challenge with a sense of purpose. As Thomas Edison replied when asked how it felt to fail while trying to invent the light bulb: "I didn't fail. I found 10,000 ways how not to make a light bulb."

Don't obsess over the annoying details. Deal with the problems, adjust and move on.

It's the stuff of life.

Chic Girl's Tip

Dressing confidently and being noticed in the clothes you've reworked isn't cause for embarrassment, though it will very likely be an invitation for questions. I go with this: If a person notices the one-of-a-kind piece you've created to reflect your uniqueness—they've paid you the highest compliment. So dust off your sewing machine, create the pretty, and wear your creations with pride.

Before You Begin

Not everything you see in the store can be attractively refashioned. Not to be negative or whatever, but let me repeat: Not everything you see in the store can be attractively refashioned. I feel it's important to acknowledge our desire to get refashion-happy along with the actual challenges a garment represents *and* to take care of both since the goal is to look unique, not like the proverbial DIY train wreck. There are massive amounts of garments with empty space to be filled, so identifying the refashion hazards before you jump right in to a project will save time and money.

Before you run off to buy every sleeveless top and mini dress you can find, you should follow a few guidelines to avoid becoming the girl who sews a $1.00 T-shirt over a satin ball gown (I've only seen this work, um . . . never). Being aware of a garment's limitations and the extent of your immediate resources is the vital component to making creations that look phenomenal. There are four (loudly screaming) clues that might hinder the probability of a garment being attractively altered or refashioned—these are fabric color, print, texture, and shape. How can you avoid the pitfalls that cause your fabulous ideas to unravel in a tattered mess? Below are some guidelines.

Color

Certain colors lend themselves to refashioning due the lack of immediate fabric availability (if you live around the corner from Mood Fabrics in New York, then please disregard that statement). There are so many shades within a color family, and each of those colors can have a different base color, which makes matching fabrics to ready-made clothes like a veritable minefield that can quickly sabotage a DIY project (which is why I'm constantly checking the lining of brightly colored dresses to see if it's the same as the outside fabric of the dress). I've made many a sleeve from the underlining of a sleeveless

Chic Girl's Tip

Empty space: How I refer to my DIY play land . . . all the missing elements of a store-bought garment that can be used as inspiration to embellish or refashion.

dress. It's not that you won't occasionally get lucky and find a well-appointed lining or perfect match to an off-shade dress. There's always the delightful exception; but exceptions aside, I've found the easiest colors to match at the fabric stores are white, gray, ivory, pale pink, navy, black, brown, blue denim, and metallic.

Check out the colors of the majority of the pieces used in this book, and you'll find many creams and neutral-shaded garments, but no matter the color, variations occur. All whites are not the same. Some are black based; others are brown based. For a finished garment that looks deliberate and chic, you'll need to check the fabric in natural light against the fabric of your garment to ensure a good match.

Print

It's more likely that you will be struck by lightning in your lifetime than you will ever find an exact print match to the garment you wish to rework. I'm kidding. Actually, no . . . I'm not kidding. When design houses choose fab-

rics for their clothing lines each season, many put a "lock" on that print to prevent fabric mills from releasing the print to other vendors. So, obviously, those great prints rarely make an appearance in your local fabric store. I love a great print, which is why I've been known to shop the clearance section and buy two dresses of the same print and borrow fabric from one of the dresses to add length or sleeves to the other. If you only have one great patterned dress, the good news is that it's totally fine to use contrast patterns or introduce a solid to the look as long as your prints have the same color scheme. You can even introduce a print to an otherwise solid-colored garment. Bottom line, a good print match is difficult to find.

Texture

A great refashion transforms a garment and makes it unique without compromising its inherent design characteristics. This is where fabric textures become really important. A bad texture match is painfully obvious (again I reference the T-shirt and satin ball gown).

Chic Girl's Tip

Check both sides of a fabric when looking for a match. The right side of a print is generally much brighter and shinier than the wrong side. Use the wrong side of a patterned fabric if the matte finish is a better match.

My point (and I do have one): It's not that you can't be adventurous. You should be—but the embellishment and the original piece must jive. Otherwise, train wreck.

If you can't find a texture that matches, look for iridescent fabrics, which coordinate with a greater range of colors since the color tone changes depending on the angle or check the wrong side of the fabrics to find a match. And FYI, it's okay to use the wrong side. I do it all the time.

In my humble opinion, it would be better to mismatch colors completely than to use a non-stretch satin along the hem of a casual Ponte knit dress. Texture is very important to achieving a finished product that is chic and fabulous.

Shape Matters

Understanding how a garment is constructed and recognizing some basic shapes will eliminate serious frustration when working toward a successful refashion.

Full Armhole vs. Strap For the projects in this book, you will want to use garments with full armholes rather than straps or inset armholes placed several inches inside the shoulder joint.

A full armhole is complete, with fabric all around the sleeve opening. For these sleeve additions to work, the edge of the shoulder fabric should reach to where the upper arm meets torso at shoulder joint or very close to that point.

The feel and look of your embellishment should match the elements intrinsic to the original garment. Even if you're deliberately using a contrasting color or texture, the tone of the technique you use should be in harmony with the initial design and the embellishments should flow seamlessly with the original piece. *Wow. That sounded way fancy and clever.* If you're working with a white cotton peasant dress, you wouldn't want to embellish with white brocade. If you're altering a knit dress, you shouldn't embellish with a fabric that doesn't stretch in the same way. If you're reworking a delicate lace dress, it wouldn't make sense to construct sleeves from stiff denim.

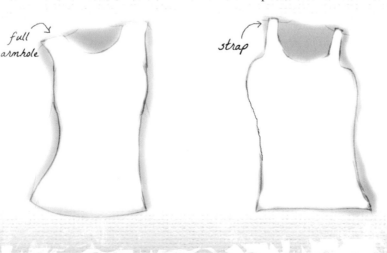

circle skirt

gathered skirt

Circle Skirt vs. Rectangle Any skirt shape can be embellished, but understanding the difference and being able to recognize these two popular silhouettes will help you decide which techniques will work best for a particular garment.

A circle skirt is fitted at the waist and flares out widely at hem. When you stretch it out flat, the hem forms the shape of a wide half circle.

A hem of a rectangular or A-line skirt will be fairly straight along the bottom edge when stretched flat even if gathered at the waist.

Bias Trim vs. Gathered Trim I always use bias trims in places where bulk is an issue. The armhole is a good example. Too much gathered fabric under the arm would be massively uncomfortable and equally unsightly.

Bias trims have dimension and fullness without additional gathering. When you lay bias trim flat, it flares at the bottom while top edge remains smooth.

A flat trim would have to be gathered to create ruffles and dimension. Ribbons are a good example of flat trims. Regular cuts of fabric can be also gathered to create a ruffled trim.

Those are the guidelines. I run every potential project through this grid. If I buy a garment with a potential problem in any of these four areas, I march (slang for "drive my red minivan") straight to the fabric store and look for a match before committing to the project. If I can't find the fabric to make it work, I return the garment to the store. It's a waste of money to hang on to pieces that are hauntingly beautiful but would never work for your lifestyle, can't be altered to fit, and don't have a snowball's chance in the desert of being attractively refashioned within the confines of your immediate resources. Save your hard-earned money. There will always be another garment awaiting the touch of your Midas fingers.

bias trim

gathered trim

Resourceful methods for making clothes
fit you and your lifestyle

PART 1

Tailor & Refashion

You don't have to go all gung ho and demolition crazy to make a garment your own. Many times all that's needed is a nip/tuck or moderate adjustment. Shopping at secondhand stores or the clearance wall at your favorite store in the mall can be highly rewarding and equally frustrating if you can't find your size (and when you do, the ketchup stain is predominately displayed). I quit limiting myself to shopping my size years ago. Dressing well and comfortably in clothes you love shouldn't be avoided because of lack of availability. The techniques in this section will help you turn off-size or off-style pieces into wardrobe essentials.

Downsize a Skirt

The most frustrating thing about shopping the sales rack of your favorite store is finding the perfect item in the wrong size (and it's inevitably the only one left too!). Skirts that are too large are a super easy three-step fix, even if the item is several sizes too big. The trick to simplify this or any downsizing project is to mark the piece while inside out. This makes the end result more accurate.

13

What You Need:

Oversize skirt

Scissors

Straight pins

Marking Pen

Iron

What You Do

1. Start with a skirt that is large or ill fitting.

2. Turn skirt inside out and mark to adjusted size.

3. Machine stitch down length of skirt following marked line as a guide.

4. Trim excess fabric away close to seam. Zigzag (see common stitches) edges if fraying is a concern. Press seam flat.

Chic Girl's Tip

If you don't feel comfortable marking a piece while it's on you, lay it flat on top of a similar, well-fitting piece in your wardrobe and mark ½ inch away from the edge. Baste (see glossary) along the line first and then try on to ensure the marks are correct. Adjust if necessary, then cut and machine stitch.

Done!

A white dress in summer always feels fresh, but the version I owned was shapeless. *Not cool.* Adding elastic at the waist (don't place it too high) confines all the extra baggage into a pretty but still relaxed shape. When adding elastic to a garment, you'll want to place the elastic band one inch lower than the point where the dress hits at your natural waist. This will give you that extra bit of bubble at the waist that frees your shoulders and torso to move about without pulling up your dress every time you raise your arms. With a bit of well-placed elastic, a shapeless dress goes from awkward to easy-to-wear.

Add Elastic

What You Need:

Shapeless garment

Elastic band 1 inch wide

Marking pen

Scissors

Straight pins

Measuring tape

Iron

What You Do

1. Start with a shapeless dress.

2. Try it on inside out and mark the natural waistline. Lay garment flat on floor or ironing board and measure from bottom hem to waistline mark, minus one inch. Use this number to mark the placement line (see glossary) for elastic on inside of dress around circumference of dress. Measuring from the bottom hem to waistline is more accurate than trying to measure down to waist from the shoulder seam.

3. Cut elastic to a length that fits comfortably around your waist, plus one inch. Pin to placement line, dividing excess fabric evenly across elastic.

4. Stretching elastic gently to fit as you sew, machine stitch band to inside of dress following your placement line. Overlap ends of elastic and stitch to secure. Lightly press.

Done!

It works with prints too.

Occasionally, you come across a dress that you absolutely L-O-V-E. You want it the way it is . . . no embellishments, no frills; but for whatever reason (maybe to be more appropriate for work or because you're taller than the average woman), you simply need a useful, longer length. If the dress you own utilizes the same fabric as a facing, you can use it to your advantage. It's an understated way to achieve some length without changing the basic look of the dress.

Facing as Length

What You Need:

Too-short skirt or dress with a hem facing (see glossary) constructed of the same fabric as the garment.

½ yard lining fabric or silk (see glossary)

Scissors

Straight pins

Seam ripper

Measuring tape

Iron

What You Do

1. Start with a dress that uses 3–4 inches of garment fabric as its hem facing. You can also create your own facing by using a similar fabric as the garment.

2. Carefully (using that seam ripper) remove the hem stitches to let the facing hang down.

3. Cut two rectangle shapes from lining fabric using same width and length dimensions as existing facing, plus one inch for seam allowances (see glossary). Machine stitch ends together to form a single, continuous band

4. With right sides together (see glossary), attach new facing to bottom of existing dress facing. Press seam allowance down. Turn raw edge (see glossary) of lining up ½ inch. Press.

5. Turn lining fabric up to inside of dress. Press. Pin into place on outside.

6. Topstitch (see glossary) along top edge of old facing to finish off.

Chic Girl's Tip

A traditional seam allowance is ⅝ inch, but when calculating for garment projects, I allow for a ½-inch seam allowance. A ½-inch is much easier (for the mathematically-challenged) to calculate than the traditional ⅝ inch seam allowance.

Done!

Tailor a Dress

Every girl needs a fabulous print dress and a bit of tailoring is all you need to transform an oversized dress into an easy-fitting dress you can grab when you want to look great without trying too hard. The key is to be moderate in the tailoring to maintain that loose, modern shape. You'll be looking for ways to make this a dress-up, dress-down essential.

What You Need:

Too-large free-shape or elastic-waist garment

Scissors

Straight pins

Marking pins

Iron

What You Do

1. Start with an oversized garment.

2. Turn dress inside out and use pins or a marker to mark stitching line. You can use another dress as a guide.

3. Baste along marked line. Try on and adjust if necessary. Machine stitch.

4. Trim close to seam with scissors and zigzag (see common stitches) edges to prevent fraying.

Chic Girl's Tip

You might need to clip some notches (see glossary) in seam allowance curves at armholes. When downsizing across multiple sizes, the fabric will sometimes bunch under the arm and a few small notches will release this tension. Don't clip too close to the stitching.

Done!

Dress into Pencil Skirt

I'm always on the lookout for great fabrics and when I spot the bling of sequined fabric all I can think is, "Well hello, sparkle." A sequined pencil skirt is a slick alternative to an ultra-trendy piece, so repurposing a halter dress into a classic wardrobe essential seems a no-brainer to me. And what girl doesn't love to don a sparkly skirt that makes her feel cool, calm, and collected? (Any garment that evokes such a feeling is a bonus for flighty girls like me.)

What You Need:

A relatively straight dress
(as opposed to a ball gown
or circle skirt)

7–9 inch zipper

Spool of 1-inch grosgrain ribbon

Scissors

Straight pins

Seam ripper

Measuring tape

Iron

What You Do

1. Start with a garment whose shape you deem useless while retaining an excessive love for its fabric.

2. Measure from bottom hem of dress to the waistline to mark length needed for the skirt. Cut away the top half so the desired length remains.

3. Using another pencil skirt you own as a guide, cut sides straight, leaving extra ½ inch for seam. Machine stitch with right sides together. If there is a lining, stitch it separately.

4. Remove back center seam with seam ripper approximately seven inches from top. If there isn't a back seam, you can leave one of the side seams open to accommodate the zipper.

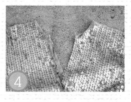

5. Using a zigzag stitch, finish off the raw edge along the top edge of skirt to secure lining and prevent unraveling. Apply grosgrain ribbon to top of skirt by placing flat on right side. Topstitch (see glossary) close to edge of ribbon through all thicknesses.

6. **Fold** ribbon to inside at back seam and tack in place with machine. Baste right sides of back seam together. Press seam flat and sew zipper into place by topstitching ¼ inch along both sides and across bottom of zipper. Remove basting. Press with warm iron (you don't want the sequins to melt after all that hard work!).

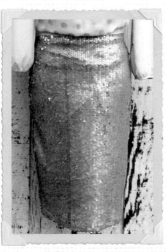

Done!

PART 2

Take On the Plunge

It's astounding to walk through the mall and find oodles of necklines with nothing. I mean, literally--nothing--no fabric, let alone embellishment. *I know.* The sheer lack is confusing, since necklines offer the most delicious opportunity for feminine detailing--flat surfaces with maximum exposure even when wearing a blazer or cardigan. It's all in the details: buttons, pleating, sequins, and ruffles. Try these techniques to give your wardrobe a jolt of feminine-infused style that guarantees effortless chic all year round.

Sequin Crush

If you—and by you, I mean me—have a closet full of nondescript items that never get worn because they lack personality, then sequins are the sort of detailing for you. With a little razzle-dazzle, this garment becomes so much more than a neutral basic—it becomes a statement piece.

What You Need:

Garment with unembellished neckline

Package of sequins

Sewing needle with sharp point

Scissors

Clear thread

What You Do

1. **Start** with a garment that screams "snooze-fest."

2. **Going** row by row crosswise, hand sew sequins to garment by coming up with thread on one side, then down on the other.

3. **Continue** row by row until you've rounded entire neckline.

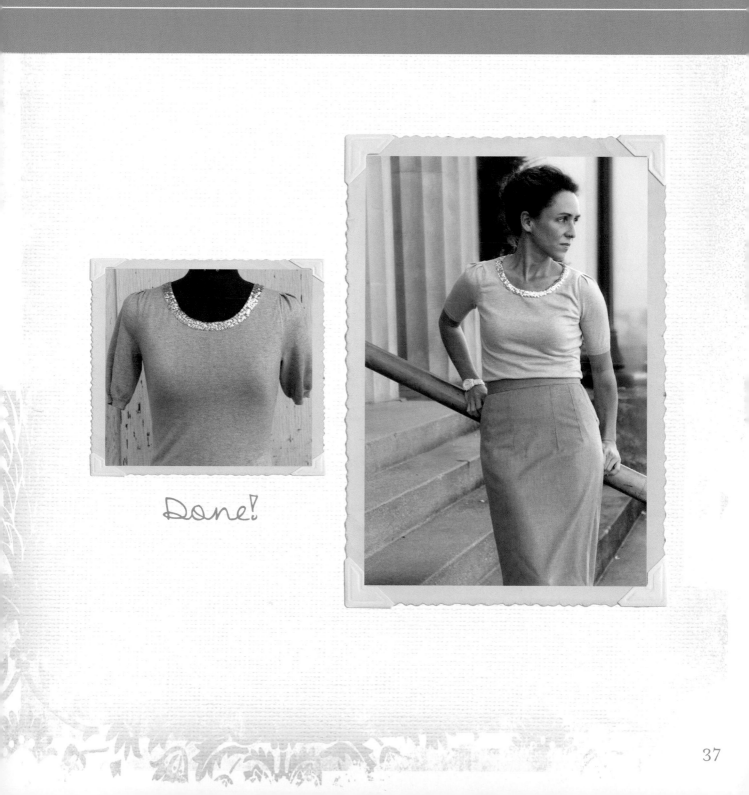

Done!

Take on a timeless military trend to raise a square neckline and create a look that's anything but stodgy. A trim row of crested buttons shows your mettle while the feminine peplum keeps it ladylike. Just what you need to flash your "Jackie-O in New York" credentials (and we all know how *that* look became a national treasure).

Military Square

What You Need:

A garment with a square neckline

½ yard matching fabric

8 nautical-inspired buttons

Scissors

Straight pins

Measuring tape

Iron

What You Do

1. Start with a fitted dress with a square neckline.

2. Using the neckline and bodice of the dress as a guide, mark and cut two rectangles that slightly narrow toward the base of bodice, allowing extra width for ¼-inch seam allowance on all sides.

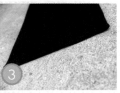

3. With right sides together (see glossary), machine stitch rectangles together with ¼-inch seam along both long sides and wide end. Leave narrow end open. Turn inside out and press crisp.

4. Place rectangle flap at desired location on dress, turning raw edge of narrow end under and stitch in the ditch to secure. (see glossary). Topstitch close to side edges to secure rectangle sides to garment. Lightly press. Attach buttons along inside of rectangle.

Done!

Bib Front

Put a fresh twist on the traditional scoop-neck dress with a sweetly buttoned-up bib front. This quirky, conversational treatment takes this piece from ho-hum to a garment that nods to vintage nostalgia. Using large tortoise buttons and leaving raw edges adds textural interest that remains cohesive to the relaxed vibe of the dress.

What You Need:

Scoop-neck garment

1 yard fabric

3 tortoise buttons ⅝ inch or larger

Shirt you own with front
neckline you love

Scissors

Straight pins and needle

Marking pen

What You Do

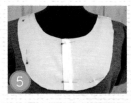

1. Start with a scoop-neck garment.

2. Using the neckline of another garment as a guide, trace the shape of a bib onto your yard of fabric. Cut shape from fabric and fold in half. Cut shape in half down the center.

3. Try the dress on and measure from the top of the shoulder down the front of the dress to determine how far down you want the bib to go.

4. Finish your bib pattern by marking the length on the edge of lower center front. Free hand the outside bib curve to the shape you desire. When you're happy with the shape, use this as a pattern to cut bib. Cut four, cutting fabric at center line one inch wider than pattern to allow for overlap for buttons.

5. Pin two pieces to dress, overlapping one inch at center to check shape. Adjust in necessary. Remove from dress.

6. With right sides together, machine stitch two pieces at neckline curve and down center using ¼-inch seam. Leave outside curve open. Clip notches at curve if needed. Turn inside out and press crisp. Repeat this step for right side.

7. Pin bib fronts to dress overlapping one inch at center. Machine stitch bib to dress "in the ditch" across shoulder seams. You will topstitch the outside curves of bib fronts ¼ from edge.

8. **Attach** buttons down center front by hand sewing through all layers.

Done!

Try this!

Mix a combination of colors and fabrics.

I've said it before and I'll say it again: A dress with ruffles will whisper its charms. There's something about ruffles that feels simultaneously natural and glamorous—like grown-up romanticism. Using fabric borrowed from the original dress is a lovely way to add interest without calling undue attention to the fact that it's been altered while creating a dreamy, fluttery effect.

Ruffles in Bloom

What You Need:

Garment with extra length at hem that can be used for ruffles

½ yard coordinating lining fabric

Scissors

Straight pins

Measuring tape

What You Do

1. Start with a garment with an unembellished neckline and extra fabric at the hemline.

2. Make a foundation for the ruffles by cutting fabric in a half-moon shape, slightly wider than dress width from shoulder strap to shoulder strap. Try dress on to double-check placement and pin so half-moon piece extends slightly under neckline of dress. Attach to dress by topstitching (see glossary) close to dress edge.

3. Cut 2 inches off dress at hemline.

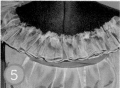

4. Divide this 2-inch length from dress into three even sections and cut. Gather each section ½ inch from top. Beginning with top layer, pin ruffle to dress, pulling gathers to fit.

5. Machine stitch gathered ruffle to dress from one shoulder strap to the other. Apply remaining ruffles so they overlap by ½ inch. Placing ruffles isn't an exact science. There's a certain amount of freedom to use your eye, rather than taking painstaking measurements.

Chic Girl's Tip

Netting fabrics, knits, and tulles won't unravel, which gives you the freedom to leave the edges raw. If you're working with a fabric that unravels easily, you'll need to take the time to finish the edges.

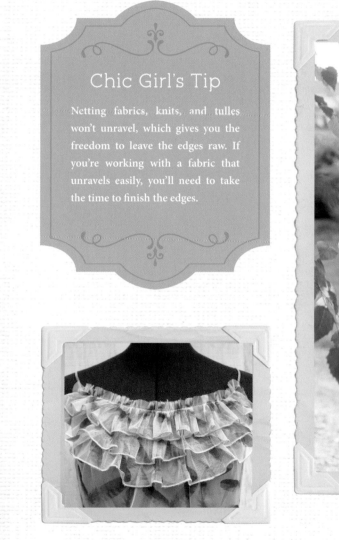

Done!

Stately Collar

Smarten up your act with a wrap-style dress featuring a structured collar and eliminate the need for a tank under your dress for good. It's a little bit working girl, a little bit class. Stand down and let this neckline make a statement for you—a dress that's ideal for work or a smart evening out.

What You Need:

Wrap or V-neck dress,
sweater, blouse, or T-shirt

Unused blouse with a stand collar

Scissors

Straight pins

Marking pen

Iron

What You Do

1. Start with a V-neck or wrap garment.

2. Try garment on over blouse and lightly mark what portion of blouse needs to be cut out.

3. Following your marks, cut the stand collar and button tab out of an unused lace or sheer blouse 1 inch wider than your marks to ensure you have enough of the collar to lay flat under the garment.

4. Pin collar into garment and topstitch (see glossary) close to edge of dress. Lightly press.

Done!

PART 3

The Brilliance of Sleeves

The impact of a sleeve can be smart, dramatic, ethereal, or flat-out fabulous. A well-appointed sleeve is like the super-sizing of a garment's original statement and so very unexpected. No other part of a garment lends itself to flamboyance quite like a sleeve addition. Sleeveless garments are readily available wherever fine clothing is sold, and these techniques will enable you to fill the empty space in ways that are equally lovely, rain or shine. The task is yours—approach with a spirit of adventure.

Sheer Extension

Whether you want a tad more length because you feel self-conscious about your arms or love the refinement of the subtle details, a sheer extension will address both. You can apply a sheer extension to a fancy piece or add a point of interest to a basic garment as I did with this sweater.

What You Need:

Garment with existing sleeve

½ yard sheer, lightweight fabric, like tulle or netting

Scissors

Straight pins

Measuring tape

Iron

What You Do

1. Start with a garment needing a touch of embellishment (only you can determine how much embellishment is appropriate for you).

2. Measure circumference of sleeve, plus one inch for seam allowance and cut a length of fabric to that length and five inches wide.

3. Machine stitch ends of fabric band together with a ½-inch seam allowance and fold in half lengthwise. Baste (see glossary) raw edges to secure.

4. Pin extension to inside and edgestitch (see glossary) close to fabric edge on right side of garment to secure. Lightly iron.

5. Repeat for other side (because it was so much fun the first time!).

Done!

Construct your own
ruffles from fabric.

Bias Ruffles

Whether your goal is to project elegance or naiveté, this is a sleeve that is full-on GIRL. Textured trims and bias flutter create a fuller shape that feels mature in spite its fairy-tale roots (we wouldn't want to look like a lost ballerina, after all). But with a flight-of-fancy sleeve, you'll never fade into the background.

What You Need:

A sleeveless dress or blouse

1 yard netting or tulle, 1 inch wide

1 yard lace trim, 2–3 inch wide

1 yard bias chiffon ruffle
trim, 4 inch wide

Scissors

Straight pins

Measuring tape

What You Do

1. Start with sleeveless garment.

2. Measure circumference of sleeve opening. Cut trims to that length plus one inch for seam allowance.

3. Layer trims with chiffon on bottom, stacking lace in middle and tulle on top. Baste through all layers to hold.

4. Machine stitch ends of trim together using ½-inch seam allowance.

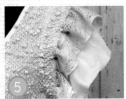

5. With right sleeve side to wrong garment side, pin layers to inside of armhole edge so ends meet at side seam under armhole.

6. Edgestitch (see glossary) close to fabric edge on right side of garment to secure.

7. Repeat for other side.

Done!

Try this!

You can fake a set-in sleeve by using any sleeve shape you want and inserting it into the armhole. Add a soft sophistication to any garment by creating a sleeve that looks like it belonged there all along. A sleeve with a slight puff (as opposed to "pouf" which conjures of disturbing leg-of-mutton images from the 1980s) is work appropriate while maintaining a ladylike charm.

Faux Set-In

What You Need:

Garment with at least a 2-inch shoulder strap.

1 yard fabric

Scissors

Straight pins

Measuring tape

Iron

Sleeve pattern with a wide sleeve cap (see glossary)

What You Do

1. Start with a sleeveless garment.

2. Cut two sleeves using the sleeve pattern of your choice or by drafting your own.

4. With right sleeve side to wrong garment side, pin completed sleeve to the inside the garment armhole.

3. Follow manufacturer's directions from pattern to construct the sleeve.

5. Edgestitch close to fabric edge on right side of garment to secure. Adjust fabric or gathers to fit.

6. Repeat for other sleeve.

Chic Girl's Tip

When applying a sleeve that drapes or is gathered, the garment's armhole doesn't need to reach to the shoulder joint (see full armhole vs. strap, p. 8). The fullness of the sleeve cap will disguise the fact that the sleeve is falling over the shoulder joint rather than from it.

Done!

Graduated Layers

I know a gossamer waterfall of chiffon layers won't solve all of life's problems, but it will make them feel relatively small and insignificant in the light of sheer DIY awesomeness. You can achieve this gauzy deliciousness by using layers of chiffon or netting to create a wearable work of art. Function *and* fashion? Yes, please.

What You Need:

½ yard each in three colors of lightweight fabric like chiffon or netting

Single-fold bias tape (see glossary)

Glue gun (without glue)

Sleeve pattern with bell shape

Scissors

Sewing pins

Measuring tape

What You Do

1. Start with a sleeveless garment.

2. Using the bell-shaped pattern as a guide, cut the bottom sleeve layer first. This should be the longest layer. Use this piece to create the next color layer, cutting the fabric one inch shorter. Repeat for third and fourth layers, making each layer one inch shorter than the previous layer. I used the same color for the top two layers.

3. Run the tip of a hot glue gun along all edges of chiffon fabric to sear and prevent fraying. Make sure you don't have any glue in the gun!

4. Baste all layers of sleeve together along top edge, then cover with bias tape. This will prevent the seam allowance of your sleeves from unraveling in a tattered mess and it looks more professional as well.

5. With right sides together, machine stitch ends of sleeve together. Press seam flat.

6. With right sleeve side to wrong garment side, pin completed sleeve to inside of armhole opening so that bias trim is not visible.

7. Edgestitch (see glossary) close to fabric edge on right side of garment to secure.

8. Repeat for other sleeve.

Done!

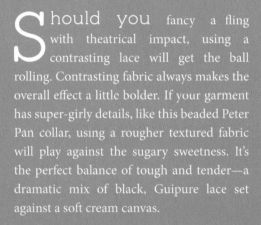

Should you fancy a fling with theatrical impact, using a contrasting lace will get the ball rolling. Contrasting fabric always makes the overall effect a little bolder. If your garment has super-girly details, like this beaded Peter Pan collar, using a rougher textured fabric will play against the sugary sweetness. It's the perfect balance of tough and tender—a dramatic mix of black, Guipure lace set against a soft cream canvas.

Contrast Lace

What You Need:

Garment with or without sleeves

½ yard contrasting fabric with interesting texture

Scissors

Straight pins

Seam ripper

Sleeve pattern

Iron

What You Do

1. Start with a sleeveless garment or you can use one with sleeves and take the sleeves out as I did for this project.

2. With a seam ripper, remove side seam from sleeve to use as pattern and lining (see glossary) for lace.

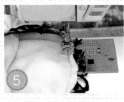

5. With right sides together, pin sleeve to armhole of dress and machine stitch to garment using ¼–½ seam allowance.

3. Cut sleeve from lace fabric. Baste through all layers along curved sleeve cap to hold together.

6. Trim excess fabric away from seam, zigzag (see common stitches) to prevent unraveling and lightly press seam allowance toward dress.

4. Machine stitch sleeve ends together using ½ inch seam allowance.

7. Repeat for other sleeve.

Chic Girl's Tip

Specialty fabrics that are beaded, sequined, or cut lace are hard to come by. Scour the clearance rack in the girl's clothing section in Target and Baby Gap for sequined T-shirts and beaded skirts that can be used to create embellishments. When you're shopping at secondhand stores, you can stock up on great embellishments from otherwise useless garments that can be used on other pieces. For this project, I used the fabric from a clearance blouse at Target.

Done!

PART 4

The Long & Short of It

Reinventing hemlines is where you can really pile on the pretties and give a garment that one-of-a-kind twist you crave. With color blocking, draping, and ruffling—there's no end to the possibilities (which could drive you nuts if you were driven to try them all). In this section, I've included the most basic techniques I use to embellish garment hemlines that have empty space ranging from two inches to fifteen. Use, adjust, or reinvent these procedures to suit your needs.

Lengthening a Garment

Chic Girl's Tip

Measure, measure, measure! A poorly measured embellishment will call undue attention to the fact that a garment is altered. Uniformity is *the* element that makes fabric layering work, whether its ruffles or flat layers. The only exception is when you're draping or deliberately using random lengths to achieve an asymmetrical look.

To lengthen a garment, follow this formula:

The Comfort Zone – Garment length
= Empty space to play with!

- Start with the length you want the finished garment to be (see *The Comfort Zone*, p. 3)
- Subtract the length of the unembellished garment

Empty space can then be equally divided into even lengths depending on the treatment you choose. For example: Twelve inches of empty space could be divided and treated with

four layers that are 3 inches long

two layers that are each 6 inches long

two layers that are 4 and 8 inches long

one layer that is 12 inches long

Being sure of the measurements *before* you begin will help to ensure your finished garment looks phenomenal.

When measuring to determine the final length needed to achieve uniform ruffles, measure only the part of the ruffle that is visible on the garment. Do not include the part of the ruffle that lies underneath the layer above. That will throw your measurement off, causing the added ruffles to be longer than the existing ruffles. Use this formula: *Width of ruffle visible on garment + 1 inch for overlay + ½ inch for hem + ½ inch for seam allowance.*

Tiered Ruffle

What You Need:

Skirt or dress with ruffled layers

1 yard fabric

Scissors

Straight pins

Measuring tape

Iron

What You Do

1. Start with a ruffled dress or skirt.

2. Cut fabric strips into length needed. On this skirt, the visible ruffle is 3½ inches long, so I cut my fabric 5½ inches long (*Formula: 3 ½ + 1 + ½ + ½ = 5 ½ inches long*).

3. Measure the bottom of skirt while lying flat and double it to determine circumference. Machine stitch fabric strips together with ½-inch seam allowance until you have 2.5 times that number. This skirt was 20 inches wide lying flat; 40 inch circumference. (*Formula: 40 x 2.5 = 100 inches wide*)

4. Machine stitch ends of fabric bands together to form one continuous band. Press bottom edge up ½ inch and tuck raw edge to inside. Hem. (It's much easier to do this before it's ruffled.)

5. Gather (see glossary) along top edge.

6. With right sides together, machine stitch raw edge of ruffle to bottom of skirt so it lays one inch under the upper layer, adjusting gathers to fit. Zigzag raw edges to prevent fraying.

7. Press ruffles flat.

Done!

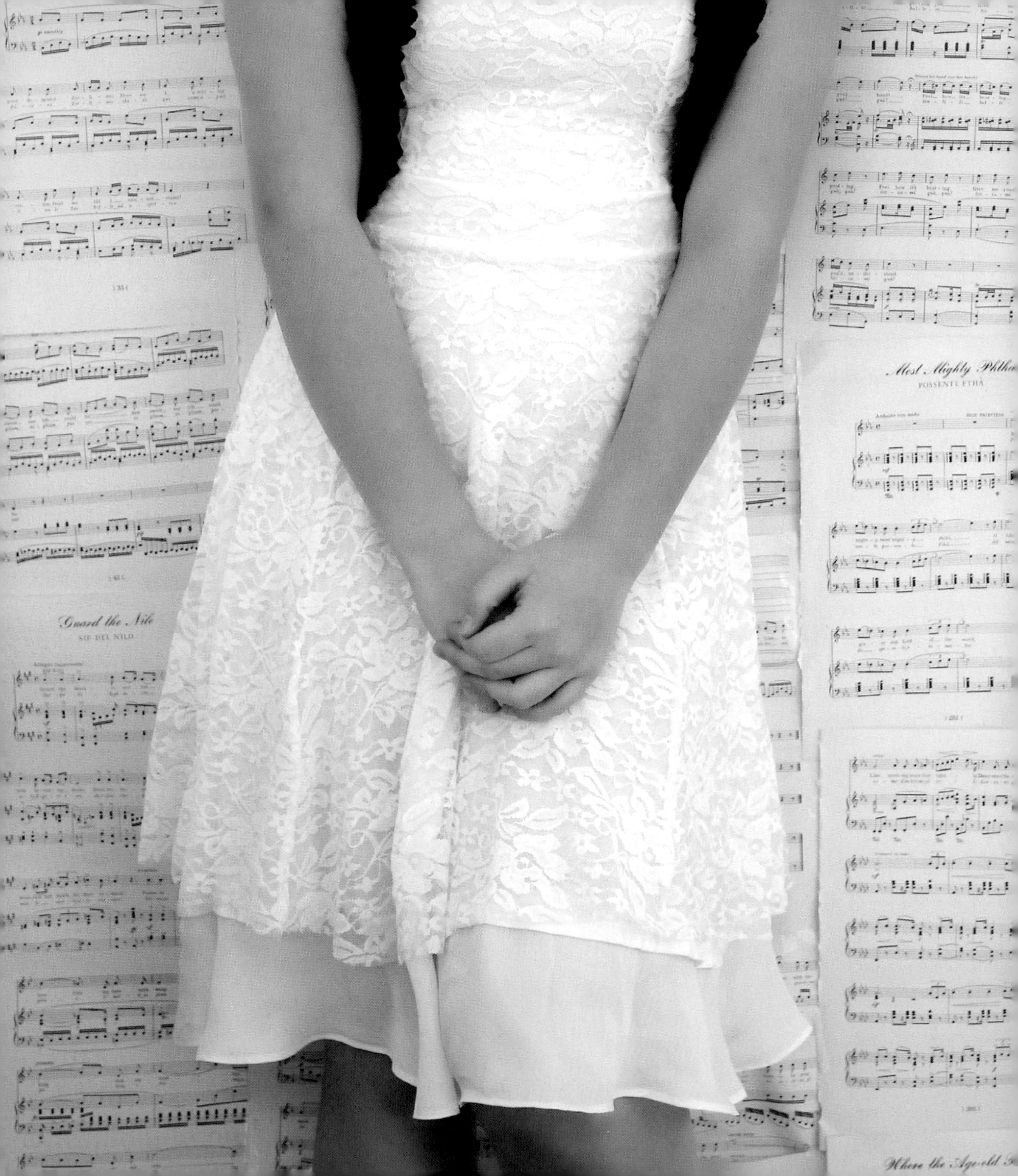
Guard the Nile
SU! DEL NILO
POSSENTE FTHÀ

Try this!

Line the entire skirt portion in a contrasting print.

When you want a hint of flutter at your hemline, an extended underlay is so much more convenient and permanent than an embellished slip. You'll never have to worry about your slip hanging too low or worse, getting yanked down to your ankles from the exuberant hug of a child. *For the record, this *has* happened to me. Two words: Never. Again. Extending the garment lining will add flutter while eliminating all potential wardrobe malfunctions. *Win.*

Extended Underlay

What You Need:

Garment with a circle skirt
(see Shape Matters, p. 8)

1½ yards lightweight fabric
like chiffon or netting

Scissors

Straight pins

Measuring tape

Iron

What You Do

1. Start with a full-skirted dress or skirt.

2. Spread dress underlay on flat surface and cut doubled chiffon to match shape of bottom edge. Using top edge of cut chiffon as a guide, measure down from the cut line to desired length of underlay plus 2 inches to accommodate a hem on the bottom and the extra allowance needed at the top where you attach it to the dress lining. This gives you a semicircle shape band for the extended piece without the hassle of drafting a pattern.

2. Machine stitch both ends together to form continuous band. Turn up and stitch ½-inch hem.

3. Pin right side of chiffon band flat to wrong side of garment lining. Machine stitch underlay to bottom edge of lining. Press.

Chic Girl's Tip

Cutting your underlay in the same shape as the dress (in this case, a semi-circle) ensures that it will hang with the same drape as the garment and ultimately, look like part of the original design. If the hem of your dress has less curve, you'd want to imitate that as well.

Done!

Building Blocks

Clothes with wide color stripes are a refashionista's dream come true. With color blocking, it's not really about re-creating a piece as much as adding some dramatic length to the existing garment.

What You Need:

Garment with wide stripes

1 yard each of fabric in 2 colors

Scissors

Straight pins

Measuring tape

Iron

What You Do

1. Start with a wide-striped garment. Remove the existing hem to eliminate bulk.

2. Measure length of color bands on garment to determine length of added bands.

3. Using garment as a guide on shape, cut band lengths on doubled fabric in both colors. Allow ½ inch on each end for seam allowance. The width should be the exact width of the existing bands on the garment plus ½ inch to allow for ¼-inch seams at top and bottom.

4. Machine stitch each color band together at ends to form a continuous circle.

5. With right sides together, machine stitch first color band to garment using ¼-inch seam allowance. Repeat for as many color bands as you choose to add.

6. Turn final band up to inside of garment. achine stitch along edge to hem. Press all seams and hem flat.

Chic Girl's Tip

Choosing fabrics that match in shade and texture to the garment is important for a project like this. Linens can be smooth or slubby (textured); solids can have a sheen or matte finish. Notice the differences and take care to match the feel of the fabric as well as the color shade.

Done!

Introduce a solid color band to a print dress

You can paint the town any shade you want with bold color combinations. Color blocking is an embellishment that projects confidence and even sheer audacity. Emerald green and coral together? *What?!* Many women cower in the face of color blocking, but fear not—if you pay attention, you'll notice that store-bought clothes *everywhere* incorporate color blocking in the design. Choose a garment with a simple shape to allow the colors to make the statement for you.

Color Smash

What You Need:

Semi-straight or fitted garment

1 yard fabric in a contrasting color

Scissors

Straight pins

Measuring tape

Iron

What You Do

1. Start with a basic garment. Remove hem.

2. Cut two bands the width of the garment hem plus one inch for seam allowance. The length can be as long or short as you need it. Stitch ends together to form continuous band.

3. With right sides together, machine stitch band to bottom of garment using ½-inch seam. Turn band down and press crisp.

4. Fold hem up to desired length and machine stitch.

Chic Girl's Tip

With your trusty seam ripper, remove the hem from the garment before adding a band. This allows your garment to flow naturally rather than hanging stiffly from the extra bulk.

Done!

Grand Ruffle

I don't know what you think when you see a shapeless ruffle standing out awkwardly from the bottom of a dress, but I'm gonna go with "not good." The secret is keeping the amount of gathering in check so the ruffle doesn't balloon out in an alarming way. If done right, a ruffled band will enhance the casual vibe of a relaxed garment. You can't have a bad day in a relaxed peasant dress.

What You Need:

Casual dress with relaxed fit

1½ yards fabric

Scissors

Straight pins

Measuring tape

Iron

What You Do

1. Start with a casual dress with a relaxed fit.

2. The ruffle can be cut into bands 8–12 inches depending on desired length. Determine how wide the band should be with this formula: *Circumference of garment hem x 2.5 = Total width in inches*

3. Machine stitch ends of fabric bands together to form a continuous band. Zigzag raw top edge of band to prevent fraying. Hem bottom edge of band.

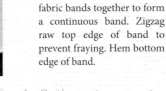

4. Gather along top edge of band (see glossary).

5. Pin right side of gathered band to wrong side of garment, adjusting gathers to fit. Topstitch close to hem edge.

6. Press ruffles flat.

Chic Girl's Tip

I always—and I mean *always*—press these large, gathered ruffles flat. It's an easy way to create a texture that looks like intricate pleating without, you know, the intricate part.

Done!

When lengthening garments with sheer fabric, lengthen the lining as well. My super-secret trick (okay, not so super secret now) is to stock up on old slips and linings from discarded garments and use them to extend the lining length of my DIY projects. It saves the time and cost of buying new fabrics, measuring, cutting, stitching, trimming, pressing . . . you get the idea. *Major time saver.*

Double Ruffle

What You Need:

Tunic or short dress

1½ yards chiffon fabric that coordinates with color of garment

1 yard chiffon fabric in accent color slightly lighter than garment

Scissors

Straight pins

Measuring tape

Iron

What You Do

1. Start with a tunic. If your garment has a bubble hem like this one, cut the elastic away and trim fabric straight.

2. Use an old slip or lining fabric to lengthen the lining to desired length. Follow instructions from *Color Smash* on page 93 to add a flat fabric extension to garment.

3. You should now have a garment as long as you want, minus the embellishments. It probably doesn't look pretty at this point, but that's okay. All we've done is create a foundation for the ruffles.

4. Measure the circumference of the new garment hem Formula: *Garment circumference x 2.5 = total width*

5. Cut the darker chiffon fabric into bands that are 8 inches in length. Machine stitch band sections together until you reach the width that is 2.5 times the circumference of garment hem.

   Formula: *Garment circumference x 2.5 = total width*

   This dress was 44 inches in circumference. I sewed the bands together until the entire width equaled 110 inches, which gave me plenty of fullness for gathers. Machine stitch ends together to form a continuous band.

6. Using a very narrow zigzag stitch, stitch along both edges to prevent fraying. This also makes chiffon fabric crinkle in a pretty way for added texture.

7. Gather chiffon band along top edge. Pin gathered band to garment so it falls just past the foundation extension, adjusting gathers to fit. Stitch to right side of garment. Keep lining free as you embellish the outside of the dress.

8. Repeat steps 4–6 with the same fabric to create another ruffle that is 4 inches long and 110 inches wide, stitching to garment so it falls just over the top edge of the longer ruffle.

9. Using the lighter fabric, repeat steps 4–5 to create the narrow accent ruffle that is 2 inches long and 110 inches wide. Make two.

10. **Gather** small bands down the center. Pin ruffles directly along the top edges of each of the other ruffles, adjusting gathers to fit.

11. **Attach** to garment by top-stitching directly down center of each ruffle on right side of garment.

12. **Lightly** press with warm (not hot!) iron. Top ruffle will fall over bottom ruffle layer.

Done!

Create a soft color palette or mix it up with bright shades

Bias Layers

Bias layering can transform an average chiffon skirt into a flippy, swishy cascade of lavish movement. It's the meeting of great architecture and romantic flounce . . . of meticulous detail with subtle dimension. You can make layers the same color or, should your fancy dictate, use multiple colors. The effect of this technique is fluid, flattering, and oh-so-ladylike.

What You Need:

Dress with skirt portion constructed from lightweight fabric like chiffon or netting

3 yards netting or soft tulle

Scissors

Straight pins

Measuring tape

Iron

Yardstick

What You Do

1. Start with a garment having a lightweight skirt portion. If the garment isn't long enough, you can extend the lining and outer garment fabric. (see *Color Smash*, p. 93)

2. This dress wasn't very long, so I lengthened the lining by using the bottom half of a black slip and added a chiffon extension to the outer garment.

3. Spread skirt hem flat and measure from seam to seam. Double the measurement to determine the circumference of the garment. Bands should be the circumference width and 6½ inches long.

4. Using a yardstick or a measuring tape, cut 4 bands on the bias that are 6½ inches long and the circumference width.

5. Machine stitch ends of one band together to form continuous band. Fold band in half lengthwise with right side out.

6. Starting with bottom layer on right side of fabric, position the raw edge of bias band toward the bottom of hem and pin it 2¼ inches from hem fold. Machine stitch band to garment using ½-inch seam allowance. Turn band down toward hem and press.

7. Repeat with three remaining bands, stitching each band 2¼ inches from the seam of previous band and turning each band down toward hem to press. This will ensure that the bottom of each layer falls slightly over the top of the layer below.

Done!

PART 5

Midriffs &
Bare Shoulders

Call me old-fashioned, but sometimes, certain styles simply aren't useful for your lifestyle or body shape or age, for that matter. The manipulation of cropped tops and strapless dresses is so . . . not done. Admittedly, a successful refashion of this sort is more difficult because of fit issues, but I choose to believe that super-trendy pieces can be the perfect canvas for more classic silhouettes. *I know, I know. I have an irrational sense of optimism.* Even advanced stitchers overlook this gold mine of potential, but should you accept the challenge, these garments just might become the most cherished in your closet.

Update a crop top with a flattering, of-the-moment peplum to create a fashion-friendly alternative. A collared blouse with a pretty peplum will become the perfect standby for the most hectic of mornings. Try it in one hue or incorporate a new color. It's fun and happy either way.

Peplum Blouse

What You Need:

Cropped top that ends approximately at natural waist

2 yards fabric

Waist measurement

Scissors

Straight pins

Measuring tape

Iron

What You Do

1. Start with a cropped top that falls at the natural waist.

2. Cut a rectangle on the bias 6–8 inches long. Formula for width: *Waist measurement x 1.5 + 1 inch = width of peplum*

3. Machine stitch ends together using ½-inch seam allowance. Fold up a narrow hem. Press flat and stitch.

4. Gather peplum along top, unfinished edge (see glossary).

5. With right sides together, pin top of peplum to bottom of blouse, adjusting gathers to fit. Machine stitch using ½-inch seam allowance. Zigzag raw edges to finish. Turn peplum down and press lightly.

Chic Girl's Tip

Measure for the peplum length carefully: too short and it's a tutu—too long and it's a tunic. The peplum should flare gently over the hips. Start with 6–8 inches and adjust for your body. Cutting the fabric on the bias will create flutter without needing a circle-shaped peplum pattern.

Done!

The inspiration may be retro, but a gilt-kissed bodice melting into a dramatically full skirt pays homage to an era ahead of its time, interweaving the fanciful with the practical. Renovate a cropped top into a mesmerizing cascade of swishy goodness and please, try not to get sentimental about it (even though it *is* squeal-out-loud awesome). It's just a dress after all. With this treatment, an everyday top becomes the every-occasion dress you can't live without.

Sequined Maxi

What You Need:

Loose-fitting top that falls a couple inches below natural waist

2 yards of netting, chiffon, or tulle

1 yard ½-inch elastic band

Full maxi skirt or dress to use as a pattern guide or a premade maxi skirt pattern

Long slip or nightdress (you can also make your own lining using the same pattern you use for the skirt portion)

Waist measurement

Scissors

Straight pins

Measuring tape

Iron

What You Do

1. **Start** with a short, loose-fitting top.

2. **Cut** an old floor-length slip or nightdress at waist to use bottom portion as a lining base for the added skirt.

3. **Using** another maxi skirt or dress as a guide, cut skirt on the fold of fabric. Cut two: one for the back portion of skirt and one for the front.

4. **Machine** stitch together at side seams. Stitch slip lining to inside of skirt at waist.

5. **With** right sides together, machine stitch cropped top to maxi skirt using ½ seam allowance. Zigzag raw edges to finish.

6. **Cut** elastic to waist measurement plus one inch. Machine stitch elastic band to inside of seam allowance at waist, stretching to fit. Overlap ends to secure.

Chic Girl's Tip

The more you stretch the elastic, the more bunched the garment will be. I stretched the elastic liberally at center front and center back, and very little around the sides of garment. This causes more gathering at center, allowing the skirt to flare out from those points. Center gathering lets the fabric fall smoothly over the hips and eliminates unattractive fabric bunching at sides.

Done!

117

Stitch a blouse yoke to inside of garment

A well-appointed bodice overlay creates a look so stunning and unexpected it speaks for itself. Clean-cut, but not too boring. Understated, but more sophisticated. (Admit it: sometimes a cardigan over a dress is just too easy!) The combination of woven diamond lace and graphic chevron print will cheerfully take you from desk to date.

Blouse Overlay

What You Need:

Strapless dress with elastic at top

1 yard fabric

1 yard fabric lining (optional)

7 inch zipper

Premade bodice yoke (see glossary) pattern if uncomfortable drafting your own

Scissors

Straight pins

Measuring tape

Iron

What You Do

1. Start with a strapless dress.

2. Use a premade bodice yoke pattern to cut the blouse overlay or draft your own by tracing a favorite blouse. Make sure to leave an extra inch in center of back yoke pieces to accommodate a zipper.

3. Machine stitch yoke front and back together at shoulder seams. Repeat for lining, if using one. Insert zipper into back yoke center seam, placing zipper ¼ inch below raw edge of neckline.

4. Pin bodice yoke one inch over top edge of dress on front and back.

5. Topstitch bodice yoke to garment, tucking zipper tail to inside.

6. Angle sleeve portion of blouse overlay down slightly so the ends meet 2–3 inches below top of dress. Topstitch (see glossary).

7. When bodice yoke is sewn to garment, the zipper should stop at top of dress like this. Trim the excess zipper tail on inside.

8. Turn raw edge of neckline to inside ¼ inch. Press and topstitch to finish.

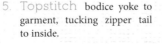

Chic Girl's Tip

Texture and pattern can make or break a project. Using a cream knit fabric would have been serviceable but less interesting. A fancy, bridal lace would have clashed with the playful vibe of the dress. This woven lace is tone-on-tone with the cream in the dress while the diamond shapes imitate the chevron color pattern. A perfect match.

Done!

Borrowed Maxi

I love dresses (massive under-statement), but there's something so unspoiled about a print maxi skirt. Ergo (using that word makes me feel all impressive and smart), the reasoning behind this project. You can have it all with this skirt—a fit that's sure to flatter with an extra-wide elastic band and a print that's as sleek as it is fun. And such a skirt is, to put bluntly, wildly awesome.

What You Need:

Strapless maxi dress in a fabulous print

1 yard 2-inch elastic

Scissors

Straight pins

Measuring tape

Iron

Extra-large safety pin

What You Do

1. Start with a strapless maxi dress.

2. Measuring from bottom hem, cut dress to a length that is 4½ inches longer than desired finished length.

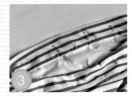

3. Fold top 2 inches of skirt to inside and press. Tuck raw edge ½ inch under for clean finish. Press and pin in place.

4. Machine stitch close to edge of waistband, leaving two inches open to insert elastic.

5. Cut elastic to waist measurement plus 1–3 inches, depending how far below your waist you like to wear your maxi skirts.

6. Attach an extra-large safety pin to end of elastic and pull through waistband of skirt.

7. Overlap elastic ends and machine stitch to secure.

8. Machine stitch remaining two inches closed, enclosing elastic. Press.

Chic Girl's Tip

When in doubt about length, go long. You can always shorten, but once it's cut . . . sigh.

Done!

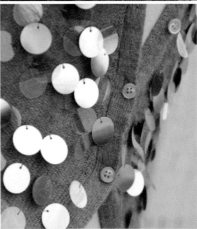

PART 6

Embellish & Create

Embellished garments and fashion accessories may seem frivolous and unnecessary, but their distinctive elements call to the princess inside . . . to that part of us quick to go on wild tangents over a few bits of cloth and well-placed beads. Hand-worked pieces often demand a high price in stores, and the fact that they're so lovely makes them hard to resist. In this section, you'll find the techniques you need to create the irresistible pretties you crave on a budget that won't empty your wallet. Secondhand stores are full of simple and inexpensive accessories that lend themselves to any interpretive flourish, whether it's graphic minimal, modern retro, or alluring charm. What better fodder for the refashionista, huh?

Floral Clutch

The floral detailing on this clutch is extravagant, mesmerizing, and little-girl-all-grown-up. Use your choice of textures like chiffon, tulle, and silk. Mix up the colors or use only one. Change your mind, then change it again. It's a woman's prerogative, no? The intricate texture of these chiffon flowers will produce a clutch that's anything but ho-hum.

What You Need:

Basic (even ugly) clutch or small bag. Mind the size. It takes a LOT of flowers to cover a small space.

Two sheets of felt

½ yard each of chiffon fabric in four colors

Sizzix Big Shot (or other fabric cutting machine) and flower shaped die

Hot glue gun

Sewing needle and thread

What You Do

1. **Start** with an unembellished clutch or small bag.

2. **Cut** felt into one inch squares.

3. **Cut** 32 flower shapes in each color, 128 total (I said it was a lot!)

4. **Layer** 3 flower shapes together. Fold in half and hand-sew through all layers of fold with thread to hold together and create dimension. You don't want your finished flowers to lay flat and tacking the bottom this way forces them to stand up.

5. **Run** the thread through a felt square and flower a couple times to attach square and form a sturdy base for flower.

6. **Repeat** steps 4–5 until flower shapes are used. I made 39 flowers to cover this 6-inch x 10-inch clutch. The number of flowers you need will depend on how big the clutch is and the size of your flowers.

7. **Apply** hot glue to the felt base of flower and attach flowers to clutch beginning at clasp.

8. **Continue** to apply flowers until clutch is covered.

Done!

Rhinestone Belt

Wrap yourself in glimmer. A grosgrain belt with rhinestone detailing is a brilliant way to add wow factor to a waistline. No matter how you style it, a rhinestone belt is sure to make you feel like you're already on holiday.

What You Need:

Spool of 1-inch grosgrain ribbon

Spool of 2-inch sheer ribbon

½ yard 1-inch elastic

Anorak Snaps and Snap Kit

18–20 large teardrop
sew-on rhinestones

18–20 medium oblong
sew-on rhinestones

About 50 small iron-on rhinestones

Scissors

Straight pins

Sewing needle and thread

Measuring tape

Iron

What You Do

FOR GROSGRAIN BELT

1. Take two measurements: the first from one side of your waist around the front to the other side. Add four inches to that measurement. This front measurement is the length of folded ribbon you will need for the embellished portion of the belt. The second measurement should be your total waist measurement. Add one inch to allow for snap overlay at ends of belt. This is the total length of the finished belt.

2. Start with layering the grosgrain ribbon over the center of the sheer ribbon. Fold both ribbons simultaneously into box pleats (see glossary) one inch wide to create texture. Pin as you go.

3. Continue until the folded ribbons reach the length from your first measurement. Secure by machine stitching close to the edge down each side leaving ½ inch unstitched at each end. Turn unstitched ends to inside and press crisp.

4. Formula to figure how long the elastic sections at back of belt need to be:

   Total waist length – front measurement + 2 inches = elastic length

   After you cut the elastic, divide and cut in half to have a section for each end of the belt.

5. Cover each piece of elastic with grosgrain and sheer ribbon by sewing evenly spaced vertical lines through both layers, leaving a small amount of give in between stitch lines to allow for stretch.

6. Insert ends of elastic portion into the open ends of front folded section of belt with exposed elastic facing toward the inside. Machine stitch through all layers to secure.

7. Fold ends of extra ribbon to back of belt and topstitch in place to finish.

8. Fit belt around waist and mark position for snaps. Following instructions on the package of Snap Kit Tools, apply snaps to ends of belt. Try a practice run on some scrap fabric.

9. Cut the bound edges of sheer ribbon away from belt and roll raw edge with fingers to create a frayed look. You can remove some of the lengthwise fibers with a straight pin to thin out the ribbon if you prefer a super unfinished look.

FOR EMBELLISHMENT

1. Starting from center of belt, mark the positions for the rhinestone design on every other raised box pleat. With needle and thread, attach the sew-on rhinestones to belt in any design you choose.

2. Place four small iron-on rhinestones between each larger rhinestone group and press with steam.

Done!

Chic Girl's Tip

If you don't want to construct the belt, you can use any premade fabric belt. Skip to the embellishment part of the instructions to create the same look.

I don't wear many sweat-shirts; okay, I might wear a baggy sweatshirt to read a book in the evening . . . when I'm too sick to do anything else, but other than that—no. If you must wear a sweatshirt to be appropriate, scatter some airy, sequined daisies across the front and suddenly its comfy-sweatshirt-meets-cozy-glam! You won't merely blip on the radar in this one—you'll blow it up.

Daisy Sweatshirt

What You Need:

Basic sweatshirt

2 yards white cotton

1 large package of silver sequins

Sizzix Big Shot (or other fabric cutting machine) and daisy-shaped die

Needle and thread

Iron

Straight pins

What You Do

1. **Start** with a basic sweatshirt.

2. **Using** fabric cutter, cut 50–60 daisy flowers. Lay them out on an ironing board, spray with starch and press to stiffen slightly.

3. **Pin** daisies to sweatshirt in random positions.

4. **Beginning** at neckline, hand sew 1–3 sequins in center of each flower, stitching through all thicknesses to secure flower and sequins to sweatshirt.

5. **Continue** to secure flowers to sweatshirt. Fill in gaps with extra flowers until front of sweatshirt is covered.

Done!

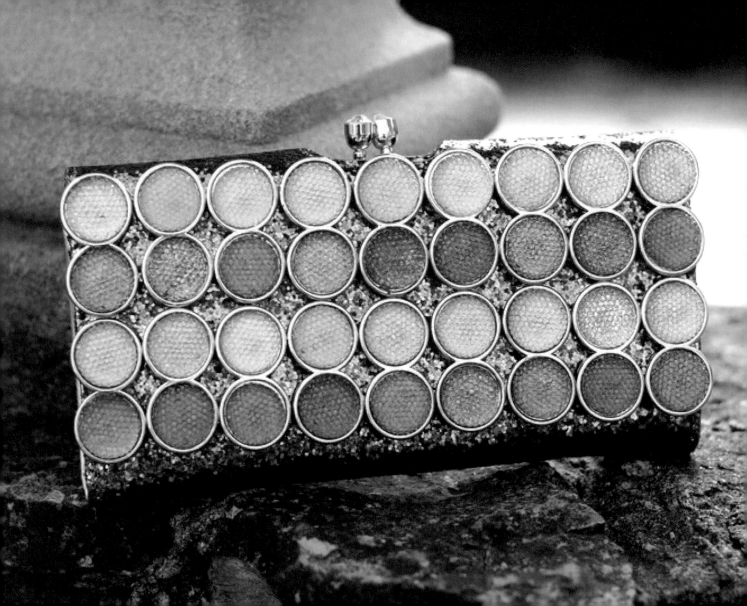

Jeweled Clutch

Y ou don't have to go all ruffles and whatnot to get your glam on. (Thought I'd clarify that. You're welcome.) With the application of a few rows of textured jewels, a hard-side clutch goes from functional to fabulous. It's always a wardrobe win to create something both fierce *and* useful . . . like specifically, a *glimmerific accessory.

*Way-beyond-shimmery-freshness

What You Need:

Basic hard-side clutch

2–3 bracelets of large jewels with flat surfaces on the back side (round jewels won't stick as well)

Hot glue gun

Scissors

What You Do

1. Start with a hard-side clutch

2. If using jewelry, cut elastic band away from pieces. Decide on a pattern before you begin hot gluing. *Just a suggestion.*

3. Apply hot glue to the back of jewels to adhere to clutch. Continue to arrange jewels in a pattern on front flap until covered.

Chic Girl's Tip

When it comes to finding the right kind of jewels, repurposing chunky jewelry is most cost-effective. Bracelets with large pieces attached by elastic are the easiest and most convenient (just cut and go). They're easy to disassemble and using larger, stand-alone pieces that are ready to glue to your bag will save the time of gluing several tiny pieces together first.

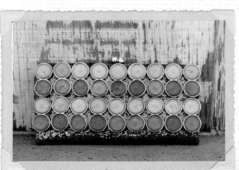

Done!

Paillette Sweater

I'll be the first to admit I have a natural exuberance (translation: unnatural affinity) for V-neck cardigans. It started out with one in every color then progressed to one in every shade of every color and now my wardrobe's pretty much a cardi-fest. (But hey, natural exuberance is supposed to be one of my endearing qualities.) Having more than one too many cardigans in my closet, I couldn't resist dressing up this classic V-neck with light-as-a-whisper paillettes.

What You Need:

Basic cardigan

1 package silver paillettes (see glossary)

1 package clear paillettes

1 package iridescent pailletes

Scissors

Needle and thread

What You Do

1. Start with a basic cardigan.

2. Starting close to shoulder, attach one paillette at a time by hand stitching and weaving thread through sweater between the paillettes. Space them 1–2 inches apart and distribute all three colors in a random pattern. When thread runs out, tie off on inside of sweater. Start again from inside with new thread to keep thread ends from showing on outside.

3. Working cross-wise toward bottom edge of sweater, continue to attach paillettes. Group them closer together as you near the middle of sweater. Begin to space them further apart toward the bottom.

4. Repeat for other side.

Done!

The Chic Girl's Official (and Not So Official) Terms

Baste Refers to the largest stitch size possible on your sewing machine (see *Gathering Stitch*).

Bias When the fabrics is cut with the corner at the top as opposed to the straight edge. The bias is at a 45-degree angle to the grain of the fabric.

Bodice The part of a garment that extends from shoulder to waist or hip line.

Bodice yoke The part of a shirt or bodice that covers the shoulders and arms.

Box Pleat A pleat in which the two parallel folds face opposite directions and form a raised box section in between.

Chic (pronounced *sheek*) Sophisticated and stylishly fashionable (I'm talking about you, of course).

DIY Do It Yourself.

Edgestich To machine stitch through all layers very close to folded edge or seam line on top side of garment.

Empty space How I refer to my DIY play land . . . all the missing elements of a store-bought garment that can be used as inspiration to embellish or refashion.

Fabric Texture This is how a fabric feels and looks and reflects light. A fabric might be smooth, glossy, nubby, patterned, matte, shiny, or coarse.

Facing Fabric turned to the inside in order to finish the edge of a garment with a fold. Facings can also function at waistline as waistbands or in places where elastic is used.

Full Skirt A garment that is much wider at the hem than at the waist.

Gathering Stitch Using the longest stitch available on your sewing machine, sew two parallel rows of stitches close to edge of fabric you wish to gather, making a reverse stitch only on one end. Leave thread tails a couple inches long on one end of stitching and pull both at same time, gently sliding the fabric along threads to create gathers that can be adjusted when inserted to waistband or sleeve opening. A gathering stitch is used to bunch fabric together.

Guipure A firm, stiff lace with no net background connected by close embroidery stitches

Leg-of-Mutton A sleeve style that is slim and fitted below the elbow, full and rounded at its cap (not a dinner dish as the name implies).

Lining A separate inner layer of material sewn onto the inside surface of a garment. The lining can be much shorter in length than the actual garment and, depending on how sheer the garment fabric is, may or may not show through.

Notch Small snips in the edge of a seam or fabric to give ease of movement or allow stretching.

Paillette A large, flat, round sequin, generally with one hole at the top to give a garment a little extra razzle-dazzle or flair.

Placement lines The lines or marks placed on fabric to indicate where design details, such as flowers, stitches, or pockets should be placed or where fabric should be cut.

Raw Edge The edge of fabric that remains unfinished.

Refashionista A creative and innovative person who transforms humdrum clothes into one-of-a-kind pieces.

Right Side The side of the fabric that is usually used on the outside of a finished garment. Colors on the right side of a printed fabric are generally stronger than on the wrong side. Unless exposing the wrong side of the fabric for a very specific reason, you will generally want to sew your seams with right sides of fabric together.

Seam The place where two pieces are joined and stitched (it holds the clothes together).

Seam Allowance The extra fabric between the seam and the raw edge.

Selvage The side edge along the length of an uncut piece of fabric

Sewn-in sleeve The most common style of sleeve, which is sewn into the shoulder seam.

Silhouette The basic flat shape of a garment.

Single fold bias tape narrow strip of fabric cut on cross-grain that is prefolded, generally used to bind the raw edge of fabric

Sleeve cap This refers to the upper curved portion of a sleeve or sleeve pattern that fits into the armhole of a garment.

Stand collar A collar that stands above the base of the neck.

"Stitch in the Ditch" Stitching that is sewn on the right side of garment directly over the completed seam stitching. This is a form of topstitching that remains hidden "in the ditch" of another seam.

Tailor To repair or alter the fit of a garment.

Topstitch stitching that shows on the outside of the garment. Topstitching is sewn parallel to an edge on the right side of fabric.

Wrong side The side of the fabric that is usually on the inside of a finished garment. There's nothing really wrong with it. The term only means it's not the top side of the weave.

Common Stitches

(1) Straight stitch As the name implies, this is the most common form of machine stitching that runs in a straight line from the beginning of seam to the end.

(2) Knit stitch A stitch used on knit or other stretchy fabrics that is slightly offset to help prevent fabric stretching.

(3) Zigzag stitch This setting on your machine creates a zigzag stitch that is most often used to finish raw edges to prevent fabric from unraveling. A very narrow zigzag stitch can be used to imitate a satin stitch on the edge of fabric often used to create a pretty finish for delicate fabrics like chiffon. This stitch was used to finish fabric for the Double Ruffle project.

(4) Blind hem stitch A specialty machine stitch used for putting invisible hems into garments.

(5) Overlock serge stitch Another specialty machine stitch that imitates the stitching of an overlock serger. Used to bind raw fabric edges together to prevent fraying.

(6) Decorative stitch Most machines come with an assortment of decorative stitches that can be used to embellish the topside of garments (much like hand embroidery, but easier!)

Resources

The fabrics and tools I use can be found at fabric stores worldwide and at these retailers.

For Materials:

Charming Charlie This store carries loads of unique bracelets and jewelry that can be used as embellishments. Plus, everything's color-coordinated which makes the perfect match easy to find. www.charmingcharlie.com. See *Jeweled Clutch*.

Clotilde An online specialty fabric destination www.clotilde.com

eJoyce Carries a large selection of rhinestone and sequin trims. See *Rhinestone Belt*.

Emma One Sock Online store with to-die-for knit fabrics in fabulous prints. Fave! www.emmaonesock.com

Hobby Lobby A large chain store full of unexpected treats for the refashionista. Print off the 40 percent off coupon available to print on their website every week. www.hobbylobby.com

Joann Fabric and Craft Stores Located across the United States and jam packed with all kinds of craft and fabric supplies. Sign up for their mailers to get great discounts and sale notifications on Sizzix fabric cutting products. www.joann.com

M & J Trimming A New York-based superstore with rhinestones, paillettes, and embellishments galore. See *Paillette Sweater*. www.mjtrim.com, 800.9MJTRIM

Mood Fabric Browse a full house of jersey knits, tulles, and laces. www.moodfabrics.com

Manhattan Wardrobe Supply A good destination for hard-to-find sewing supplies www.wardrobesupplies.com, 212.268.9993

Purl Patchwork This website is full of lovely, lovely fabrics. www.purlsoho.com, 212.420.8798

For Clothing:

Forever21 My go-to store for a huge selection of affordable, feminine pieces ideal for customizing. www.forever21.com

H&M On-trend clothing perfect for DIY projects. www.hm.com

Lulus A website full of pretty, feminine, easily customizable garments. www.lulus.com

Modcloth An online destination with more pages of 35-inch dresses than you could ever scroll through in one sitting. www.modcloth.com

Plato's Closet Recycle and repurpose gently worn clothing. www.platoscloset.com

Ruche If you hanker clothing with a vintage vibe, this is the store for you. www.shopruche.com

Target Buy the basics then bedazzle and razzle-dazzle them to reflect your personal style or find great deals on sequined and textured pieces that can be used for embellishing other garments. www.target.com

T.J. Maxx Save money and brag about your designer duds at discount store prices. Great for finding "blank-slate" pieces for DIY style. www.tjmaxx.com

About the Author

Kristina Clemens was born to an avid seamstress and built her first garment for competition at age ten. Regrettably, she did not win. Not so regrettably, this garment perished along with the rest of her clothes from the 1980s. Kristina is likely to refashion any piece she buys, and approximately 37 garments have died for the sake of her experimentation. She and her sewing machine reside in central Indiana along with her husband and three children. She is the author of the book *After Nathaniel*. You can see more of Kristina's fashion projects at www.kristinaclemens .blogspot.com or say hi on Twitter: @createclothes.

Credits

Photography Credits

All instructional photography by Kristina Clemens.

Janelle's Look Nook
Stately Collar, Building Blocks, Double Ruffle, Borrowed Maxi
www.janellespics.com
Anderson/Muncie, Indiana

Holly B. Photography
Bib Front, Grand Ruffle, Rhinestone Belt
www.facebook.com/Hollybphoto
Cincinnati, Ohio

Product Contribution

Missy's Stitch N Sew
Beanie Cap, *Paillette Sweater*
www.missysstitchandsew.com

Red Envelope
Watch, *Stately Collar*
www.redenvelope.com

Firmoo Eyeglasses
Eyeglasses, *Stately Collar*
www.firmoo.com